—— The ——
Decision

Paul R. Wiesenfeld

READERS QUILL
AGENCY
Where Every Story Finds Its Stage

THE DECISION

This is the story of Alan Gompers having to make a life-altering decision. A decision of such magnitude that it is now simply known as "The Decision".

On a startlingly clear spring day in 1981, Alan drove his brand, new Cadillac Eldorado onto his estate believing he was home safe. Sure, he had a rough day but it was also exciting, challenging and just dangerous enough to give him the constant thrill he needed. I got this figured out, he thought. No one knows where I go, what I do or how I do it.

Just as he stopped the car and opened the door to get out, he heard the screeching of tires, then the blaring of sirens. Suddenly, a police officer was screaming at him "put your hands on your head, get on the ground" and then the words he feared the most, "you're under arrest". Then he felt a gun butt jammed against his head. Only this time, it was not a police officer but a very large and angry detective who started speaking to him in a sneering vulgar manner. "We got you sucker; you're going away for the rest of your sorry life. Don't move or I'll splatter your brains all over this car".

The warm spring day turned into a dark cold winter night. The outside temperature of 68 degrees seemed to drop to ice cold, His whole body shivered. Fear, an otherwise unknown companion, suddenly engulfed every fiber of his being. This new companion spoke to him in a calm, clear yet unequivocal voice" I will be with you Alan, all the time now, wherever you go, no matter what you do or who you're with".

Alan knew one day this could happen but the drugs he took, then sold, spoke to him, saying, "don't worry you won't get caught, you're too good, you're too smart, you're safe, just keep using and everything will be all right".

In a crisis like this, time slows perceptively. However, Alan realized his worst nightmare was coming true and time began to speed up so much

he could hardly breathe, think, or see clearly. All he knew was that some very strong detective was commanding him now to put his hands behind his back and to put his face on the hood of the car. The demanding tone of this detective, as well as the gun placed to Alan's head so immobilized him, he simply obeyed.

As the handcuffs were clasped on his wrists, a strong hand pushed his face to the hood of the car. Alan heard the detective say "don't move, just listen to me". Alan tried to calm himself, but the effort was useless. The detective, believing he had accomplished his goal, turned Alan around so they were face to face. He looked at Alan as if he were a piece of trash ready to be discarded and said, "we got you shit bag". After moving in closer to Alan's face said, "you're nothing but a fucking drug dealer, you're going to jail for the rest of your life", yeah, the rest of your life".

They looked at each other, eye to eye, then the detective released his grip from Alan's throat collar and smiled as if all this was over and said disingenuously "do you understand what I just said?" Then the detective paused, looked Alan in the eye (harder than before), and suddenly screamed at him, with his face just 6 inches from Alan saying, "do you"?

Alan was so startled by the sound of the detective's voice, that he tried to recoil in horror but as his back was against the hood of the car, no movement was possible. His mind suddenly broke free from the fog of fear and a clarity of awareness descended upon him the likes of which he had never known. His heart, all the while beating like a drum, slowed to a gentle tapping. His thoughts, which were once racing now slowed to a gradual murmur. Yes, he said to himself, I understand, I know exactly what is happening to me.

Alan did not respond verbally to the detective's entreaties, he merely obeyed.

Alan knew something worse was coming because the detective gave it away by smiling and releasing his grip. Alan, he said, "your life is over. You have, no chance to escape. You're mine. The future for you is jail where they will make you "a bitch" so get used to nothing but pain and suffering".

The detective thought he knew what the impact would be to Alan as he had done this several times before and gotten the results he wanted. He paused for effect, looked at Alan and said (this time in a calm measured voice) "Do you want this? Is this what you want"? without saying a word, with the steadiness of his eyes only, Alan communicated with the detective, implying "go ahead, tell me, I'm ready".

The detective moved in closer and whispered in his ear so the other police officers could not hear "If you give me the name and address of your supplier, we can make a deal. If you accept it, you can go home now, you will be free, no jail". Oh my God thought Alan What to do? Alan was given a choice-- one he never thought he would ever have to make and now he had to decide what to do. The detective wanted him to decide right now.

Alan wanted to say just what the detective wanted to hear. He wanted to end this traumatic situation as quickly as he could. Yet something somewhere deep inside him said wait a minute hold on, be silent there may be another path to follow. The very thought of going to prison for the rest of his life was a torment he thought he could not bear but at the same time, he also knew something

might happen to him if he gave up the name of his supplier.

He imagined his wife coming over and saying. Alan, I love you, I want you to give the detective what he wants. This would be too easy he thought but yes, he so much wanted to take her advice. Troubled, he thought of Wisey--his good friend, and wanted to ask him but he was not offered a phone call or even the advice of a lawyer.

As these conflicting thoughts were waging war in his head, there was a slight movement of the detective's body and he said "Oh, I should tell you, dirtbag, you have the right to remain silent, and anything you say can and will be used against you. You also have the right to a lawyer and if you cannot afford one, some public defender will help you out". At that very instant,

Alan had the answer he needed. I'll ask for a lawyer and remain silent. This will give me time to think. He knew he did not have a lot of time but at least he was given some time and he needed all the time he could get.

HISTORY AND BACKGROUND

To appreciate the how, and the why which led Alan to make the decision he made, we first have to understand who and what he was growing up. He grew up in Parkchester, "da Bronx" in the 40's and 50's. Parkchester was an all white middle-class, Italian, Jewish and Irish neighborhood. His parents, as were every parent in Parkchester, struggling economically.

Parkchester was a considerable upgrade from the tenements which most of Parkchester residents came from and was a huge complex of apartment buildings, parks and playgrounds all built by Metropolitan Life Insurance Company. It was a safe secure and friendly envirnment with good schools, Churches and small stores in the neighborhood.

Alan's performance in just about everything he tried was barely average. He was somewhat popular amongst his friends, but otherwise, average in sports, and school work. The only talent he demonstrated which set him apart from the other kids, was in music. In this category, he was so good, he was accepted at the High school of Music and art, in Manhattan.

In the early 50's, "doo wop" music became the rage and as it turned out, Alan could sing, and harmonize with other singers. He even formed a group of "doo wop" singers who sang in the moonlight, on street corners and in High school halls. The "Moderniers" was the name of his group but managed to get one, semi-hit. Agents in those days knew how to take advantage of singing groups for their own profit. And because of that exploitation, the Moderniers made very little money while the agent or and producer got it all.

TRAIN RIDE

The first real glimpse we get into who and what Alan was, occurred during the train ride he Wisey and Billy took in the summer of '54. The three teenagers rode the subway from Parkchester, "da Bronx" to lower Manhattan, where they had summer jobs at the New York State Insurance fund.

Just sitting on a train for an hour until it stopped in lower Manhattan was boring and uneventful. The ride offered no excitement, no drama and no surprises for the young teenage boys. Alan, all of 16 at the most, looked for something to do or he thought he would die of boredom and find it, he did.

In those days, the rear door of the train closed with a rubber stopper at the end. Alan, seeing this and realizing its elasticity, tried to put his hand out of the door through the rubber stopper. He was successful. No one had ever thought to do this, but Alan saw his chance to create some mayhem and told Wisey and Billy of his idea for a prank.

As the train they were on pulled away from the stop, some people were 1. eft. standing on the platform waiting for the next train to come along. s were reading newspapers. Alan stood by the rear door and stuck his hand out through the rubber stopper and pulled a newspaper "out from" someone's hand while they were holding it upright. The train pulled away with their newspaper flapping out from the rear car door. The look of astonishment and bewilderment on the face of the person who just had his newspaper snatched, sent gales of laughter to Alan, Wisey and Billy. What could the person do? Suddenly, they had no newspaper and no way to chase after the train as it pulled away.

THE FIGHT

As summer ended and school started for the 3 teenagers, each went to a different High school. Wisey went to James Monroe, Billy went to The Bronx High school of science, and Alan to the High school of Music and art. All 3 teens had a lot in common but were different in several respects- Billy was the smart one, Wisey the athlete, and Alan the musician.

One day in early September an Irish kid in Wisey's English class for no discernable reason picked a fight with him. He did it most likely because Wisey was Jewish. Wisey was not a tough kid or one who looked for trouble. The Irish kid however lost the fight , told his older brother who came up to wisey in order to avenge his Younger brothers misfortune. The older brother who was in a gang was bigger, and stronger than Wisey, and when he saw Wisey, he realized an opportunity for his gang "The archer street Thugs" to challenge a bunch of Jewish kids to a "Street fight", which he knew his gang would win.

Wisey had no gang, was not interested in fighting but was shamed by the challenge and knew he had to go or be labeled a coward. He asked his friends to come and defend him but one by one, they offered the lamest of excuses, "I can't go with you", "I have to watch TV", "my mother said I can't get my new shirt dirty" and the most popular, I have to study for a test".

At the appointed time and place, Wisey believing he would be alone showed up. Then to his surprise only one person came there to help defend him and that person was Alan. He walked Up to Wisey didn't say a word and just stood at his side. They stood shoulder to shoulder at the appointed place and time as the dreaded Archer street thugs came forward. It seemed to Alan and Wisey there were at least 10,000 of them. However, since it was only Wisey and Alan, the fight to be was so unfair, so unsupportable, the Archer Street Thugs did not know what to do. They could not just go home and be shamed by two little Jewish kids. They had to do something, but what?

When the biggest of the older brothers stepped forward and challenged Wisey to a fight by pushing him ,iit was Alan who immediately reacted by punching the guy in the nose. This started a free for all with all 10,000 Irish kids jumping on the two of them. Luckily the Parkchester security police, the Good Humor ice cream man and a street cleaner came by and broke up the melee. Alan and Wisey ran home to Wisey's apartment where his mother comforted them with praise and condolences.

News of Alan's bravery spread like wildfire among the Parkchester residents. He became the talk of Parkchester in general and the teens' parents in particular. Everyone knew only Alan had the courage to come help Wisey. Only Alan stood by Wisey's side. Alan demonstrated a fearlessness, a bravery, and a courage no one else had. Alan stood out among all of Wisey's friends. He was a hero of epic proportions in the eyes of the other teenagers .

Why did Alan show up while none of Wisey's other friends would?

Why did Alan stand with him and defend him when no one else would? What made Alan come knowing how dangerous this situation could be? He was willing to face the Archer street thugs having no regard for his own personal safety? All Alan knew was that wisey his friend needed him.

Something deep and profound within him was expressing itself and no one, let alone Alan, knew what it was. The answer as to why he came to Wiseys side, when no one else would, portends the dramatic making by Alan of "**The Decision**".

FIFTEEN YEARS LATER ALAN AND A NEW FRIEND ENTER THE STOCK MARKET

The 15 years following "the fight" were quiet, if not dull, for Alan. He did not find himself or a direction that would give him anything close to the excitement he had in the fight. He graduated from Hunter College (barely) and then taught physical education on a High school level, worked at the Catskill mountains in the summer and seemed destined for a normal, safe, easy life until his new friend Howie, saw something in Alan that he wanted and needed so he did all he could to persuade Alan to join with him in the stock market. Eventually he was successful.

Howie was the moving force here but Alan carried his share of the load. They were not gifted
analysts of market trends rather they were great at "selling". And selling stocks was just what they did. Eventually, they were so good they became partners in a small over-the-counter stock- company. Now they had not only a lot more money but status and control. It was at this time that Howie figured out how they could make a lot more money very quickly, but wrongfully.

Together operating in the manner and method they preferred they made a small fortune. They accomplished their goal of making. A lot of money by cheating and scamming clients, friends and family alike. Money rolled in the likes of which Alan could only dream of. But while he was getting very comfortable financially, and seemingly having "it" all, he was losing his boundaries, his self-respect, and his friends. He could not trust anyone anymore as everyone it seemed to him only wanted his money not his friendship. He only had one friend—Wisey—who while geographically separated, was largely unaware of how Alan and Howie made so much money. He like so many others stood in awe of Alans financial success.

Making so much money brought with it the excitement Alan craved however, it also brought home something new and unexpected. He was losing his bearing as well as his moral compass. It seemed to him that while gaining material things he was now more and more alone and worse not himsel. Yes, he had new and better cars and moved from an apartment to a huge home but the cost seemed to be to his self worth. Were the two processies somehow someway connected?

His marriage and kids were secondary, but they did provide some comfort and stability to the downward path he was on. Yet, no amount of money or property could stem the slide he was on . The path to financial success was far too easy, too available but at the same time he knew it carried risk. Unseen but now suddenly felt was something new and incredibly powerful "fear".

The more money Alan made the worse his inner life became. Sure he had new and better cars, took lavish vacations and a huge home but his center, his inner sense of purpose was diminishing as rapidly as he was getting rich. It seemed to him that he could not stop doing what he was doing even though it was now ever so clear something was terribly wrong. Alan you see was getting empty at the same time he was getting rich.

Howie was very good in this racket and showed Alan how to steal, how to cheat and use others for financial gain all the while convincing him that no one knows what we door how, so not to worry no one will catch us. It all seemed too easy, too good to be true and sure enough it was soon to become the worst nightmare of his life. Alan wanted to stop he knew something was wrong but with Howie's influence and the huge amounts of money coming in Alan chose to look away. Deep down he wanted to stop doing what he was doing ,but with Howie's influence controlling the situation he just went along.

He knew deep down inside they could not keep getting away with what they were doing and sure enough one day the attorney General of NY came knocking at their door. The knock was a hard one but just and fair.

PLEADING GUILTY

This criminal matter, a first for Alan and Howie, was traumatic to be sure, but Howie assured Alan that they could do with the Judicial system what they had done in the stock market . He was confident they could beat the rap. The inner sense of right and wrong that should have guided Alan and controlled his willingness to go along with Howie was lacking. Unfortunately, as it turned out they did beat the rap as they only got probation, a fine and 10 hours of ethics training. Neither he nor Howie learned the needed lesson.

Alan knew, deep down inside that something was wrong and that something whatever that something was would manifest itself somehow, someway to him. He was right and that something did but not until later. He and Howie decided to take some time off and in this time off period looked for a new venture, one with promise and one in which they could use their selling skills. Then one day Howie said," I found it". What Howie found for them was a new and better way to make money only this time do it "legally".

Howie told alan what it was and said, it's legitimate and legal and with our skills we will do better than we did before. Howie said selling "time shares" is perfect for us. They did and sold them to the unsuspecting and the vulnerable. Howie was right, and they were more successful here than in the stock market. The financial fortune Alan thought he wanted and needed was there for the taking but so was tragedy and misfortune. He just didn't know it or see it.

While Howie was perfecting the manner and method they were to use in order to fleece the greedy, the unsuspecting the time share gullable Alan in order to ease the internal anguish he was feeling and stem the onrush of this new and profoundly powerful entity "fear" began to dabble in drug use. To him drug use was minor and temporary. It provided him so he thought with the relief he needed from the internal pain he was in. Again looked away and when he did he was not too concerned about the consequences of his action. Oh, how wrong he was to look away, as drug use was the exact opposite of what he should do. What he needed to do.

The initial relief drugs provided for his mental pain and suffering was a false flag, a false message. Hey, Alan said the drugs, take more of us and you will feel better and perform better. Nothing is wrong here. Listen to us- we are the answer. Yes, said Alan. I'll listen to you and do as you say. Getting addicted to a drug or several drugs is not what alan thought would happen and profoundly not what the doctor ordered or what he should do.

At this point in time little did he know how dangerous and consequential his drug involvement was but continue on was his modus vivendi. And so he continued. Alan seemingly unaware of the consequences he created and the ones that awaitedhim did what he was doing and gave it no more thought.

The guilt and shame (particularly shame) of what happened to him was bad enough but the why was of such proportion and magnitude as to be incurable by any drug. Getting addicted was the easy part recognizing what the problem was and why he had this problem the hard part. Finally knowing what to do to cure the problem how to do it not to mention why was almost impossible.

The answer although elusive was clearly not in drugs or making money but in finding the cause of the problem, then having the courage to go to the cure.

The worst and most important consequence Alan created for himself would be the cosmic ones. They were particularly hard to fathom, to understand then to cure. Yet they were coming at him with a vengeance and a power the likes of which he had no appreciation. It did not take long before Alan realized the road he was on was going in the wrong direction, leading him down, not up but how do I get off this road, this path and then how do I get on the right road? Where is my road map/ my direction guide book when I need it he wondered? What "is" the cause of me taking this path? Why did I do what I did he wondered?

 It was me who did it and me who has to cure the problem. If I got myself into it I have to get myself out of it. Very soon he would know the answers to these most intriguing questions just not yet.

Fortune was once again on their side. The venture into time-shares proved to be incredibly successful. They made more money here legally than they did before illegally. The problem was that selling time shares was a boondoggle for the unsuspecting, the gullible and the innocent.

Alan realized that this process of scamming the gullible was not who he is or who he wanted to be. Slowly at first then with more intensity he began to punish himself in the false belief he could thereby atone for his sins. This notion while meant well is not the answer in fact far from it. Unfortunately for him it created more pain and more suffering. He was losing his mind his soul and his heart and worse he did not know what to do or how to stop the process from unfolding.

The simple solution of taking a drug for pain relief was there for the exploration. Sure, taking an aspirin tablet works but it does so temporarily as it does not address the cause of the pain. Until this cause is understood and appreciated no amount of aspirin will cure the underlying problem. Taking a drug to ease mental pain works only temporarily but it does not address the cause but drug use is addictive and as such only makes the problem what ever it is much worse.

The more drugs Alan took the more he needed. He more he needed the more he had to buy and buying drugs consistently was not something he could hide. The police, detectives as well as special groups within the law were onto this situation having encountered a great many others in this predicament.

People in pain usually do not think rationally or carefully they are only interested in the ending of the pain. Alan did not know on a conscious level that the scamming he was involved in with Howie was the cause of his problem or that it created consequences for him that were out of his control. He did not think that he could stop taking drugs or that he would get caught only that the pain he was in was intolerable.

Alan not sure what to do or how only that something had to be done decided to leave Howie and his I influence over me, the time share racket and I'll head out on my own. It was a momentous decision on his part and the path to success dubious. He saw an opportunity for him to buy a nightclub and thought this could work. At the same time he found an opportunity to get into the boxing racket with a fighter. Both were opportunities for him and both called on his skill and talent as an entrepreneur but he was still alone in pain and had no experience in either field.

He did have a companion however the one he dreaded the most "fear". Fear was his constant companion and incredibly powerful. Little did he know that this companion an unseen and silent. Companion would be his undoing. The more mental anguish Alan was in the more he thought he needed drugs to ease the pain. Tthe uncertainty as to where he was going and why was overwhelming.

As his troubles grew so did his drug use. Both opportunities night club ownership and boxing were just that opportunites but they proved insufficient to stem his downward path. This change of direction did nothing to slow the onslaught of what he created for himself. It did not take long before the drug use caught up with him and low and behold gave rise to **"The Decision"**.

EVALUATING HOW AND WHY TO MAKE THE RIGHT DECISION THEN MAKING IT

Getting arrested for using drugs was the minor offense charged. The more serious and the more onerous one was that of "selling" drugs which carried the greatest fine and most time in jail; 15 years to life in prison. It was this one that caused Alan the most concern and only exacerbated his already present "fear".

The undercover squad was on to him as they had eyes and ears all over the drug community. Alan had no idea he was being followed or tailed or watched over.

It took some time after getting arrested for events to play out as they should and in it Alan had time to think. It was in this 'thinking" period of time that Alan realized what meditation had to offer and how helpful it could be in his situation.

Alan knew he was on a precipice- he had. Everything one could want and he could lose it all. His first step in heading off the tragedy he was involved in was to get a lawyer, a good criminal defense attorney who might be able to help him avoid the worst. Alan paid this person a lot of money and thought I better get what I paid for but oh how disappointed he was.

After speaking with the state and reviewing the evidence the great defense lawyer who took a huge sum of money said to Alan they got you stone cold. I cannot win this case for you but I can get them to allow you not to go to jail, to keep. Your money and home and all you have to do is become a snitch and give up the supplier. You win and you can walk away a free man keeping all that you have. So easy said the lawyer but what the lawyer did not know is that Alan knew him. Had done something wrong and that something was not right with this deal no matter how much he wanted to take it.

It was not just his lawyer who said plead out "stay out of jail" his wife pleaded. Do this not just for me but for the kids we need you here with us not in jail. Her argument was Oh so persuasive and he loved her but something deep inside him and said no do not give up so quickly something is wrong here.

judge on the day of trial said, if you plead guilty I will not put you in jail as I am aware of the state's offer. All you have to do is give up the name of the supplier of the drugs you bought and sold. That's all and Alan if you won't do this I will have no choice but to go along with the state's recommendation and send you first to Rikers Island then to the Eastern Correctional Institution for 15 years to life.

judge on the day of trial said, if you plead guilty I will not put you in jail as I am aware of the state's offer. All you have to do is give up the name of the supplier of the drugs you bought and sold. That's all and Alan if you won't do this I will have no choice but to go along with the state's recommendation and send you first to Rikers Island then to the Eastern Correctional Institution for 15 years to life.

As it turned out Alan had 5 months to think about what decision he should make. He needed all 5. He could not have imagined so momentous a decision as this one. If he asked 1,000 people, all but one would have said turn on your supplier, 999 would have said take the deal and get away with it all. Going to jail is too dangerous, too risky and too frightening for you.

ALAN'S PROPHETIC SAYINGS

Alan found the answers he was searching for in meditation. This came as a surprise but nevertheless it was in meditation that the clarity and vision he needed found its way first to his head-mind then to his heart. It was in the heart that Alan found the state of inner peace he so coveted. Then the path took him to God and finally love. He knew from the experience he had that God and man are not separated that God does not dwell in the heavens above rather God dwells in the heart of man.

When he meditated the clarity and vision, he sought brought with it the elusive state of inner peace and contentment that was previously lacking. It did not take long for him to realize he was the cause of his own demise. It was not Howie, or his parents it was he-himself that caused the problem. The problem was therefore not out there in someone or something. It was me and me alone that created the pain and suffering I suffered from and therefore no drug no beverage no other could touch it.

This astonishing realization also provided the answer for him to what he was searching for but could not find in drugs, sex and rock'n roll. The answer was uncomfortable to be sure but, in the answer, he found the power to change to grow to perfect his new condition. If indeed he was the cause he was therefore the cure.

The issue presented for his consideration was to be a snitch or not be a snitch were severe, for sure but in his new state, where he was free and at peace with. Himself, those consequences were not to be feared as they were before. Alan now was on the path to not only knowing the right thing but to have the courage and confidence he never had before to do it.

Follow righteousness and truth and you will not go wrong. Go with this new sense of freedom he reasoned now and I will lose my constant companion- fear. It was this fear that retarded his groth and development and prevented him from seeing clearly. It was fear that prevented him from being free. This fear factor kept him in the dark alone and frightened.

The answers were revealed to him in the meditative experiences he had and the answers were what set him free. Freedom is not bought in the department store or given by charities it is something that comes from God, from within from being open and honest with oneself.

Sometimes the simple, the obvious is the answer even if it does not at first seem so. Alan allowed the light to shine on him. He was walking in the sunshine even when it was raining. He was free even when he was behind bars. He was now at peace with himself and all of mankind.

Let's look at Alan's 4 provocative sayings now and see if we do not agree with him.

1. We create what happens to us.

If something bad happens to us we usually find a reason not to accept responsibility rather we seek to blame it on another or God or our parents. No this is not the solution because what happens to us whether we want to believe it or not is caused by our actions. We may be afraid of the consequences and therefore not want to think we created the problem but we did.

2. Judgement creates separation.

No one wants to be judged by another. When we are so judged too often, we are found wanting, wrong at fault. That's why we do not want another to judge us. Once we are judged the judgment so made can be limiting or worse, we are made to feel irrelevant. Therefore, when we are judged by another an invisible wall is created. Even if we don't see it it's there. Even in the bible, it says do not judge lest ye be judged.

3. We are all one.

Of course, we are all different in size color race and religion but these differences are not determinative. There is no one race that is superior to another by virtue of it being white, black, brown or yellow. No religion that is the only true religion. To Alan we mankind no matter where we are from, our color or sex. we are all one its what we make of our talents our education and our skills that determines whether we will succeed or not.

4. Blame

As there is no other than there can be no one to blame. Simple clear direct and accurate. Try getting away with blaming your parents, your government your neighbor and see what happens? War miserere and loneliness.

THE DECISION AND ITS CONSEQUENCES

After considerable a particularly insightful meditative experience some thought and introspection, Alan decided what the decision he had to make should be and why.

He reasoned that If I am to be honest with myself I must accept responsibility for what I did. To be a snitch is not being honest with myself or accepting responsibility. In fact if I snitch it could Just as well create far worse consequences for me. He decided not to be a snitch, a rat and or a squealer. He chose instead to face the consequences of what he did.

On the day set for trial he was asked by the Judge how do you plead? guilty or not guilty? not guilty would cause a trial to be held. The evidence of guilt as the detective said was overwhelming. It was and a jury found Alan guilty.

After a meditative experience, Alan knew what decision. He would make. Sure, his lawyer told him if he did not snitch. And he elected to go to trial he almost certainly would lose as the evidence was overwhelming against him. His wife pleaded with him to snitch as she said she wanted him. Home with her and the kids.

On the day of the trial when Alan had to announce his decision the courtroom was packed.

When the judge convened the court and called. Upon Alan to announce his decision the silence was deafening except for the song by Simon and Garfinkel "the sound of silence that seemed to be playing for everyone to hear except that the sound of silence was all that could be heard.

Alan would not be a snitch. He was not about to tell who his supplier was. He decided I will accept the consequences of my decision. Knowing how little chance I have of prevailing will do what my heart tells me is the right thing for me.

Then with everyone's eyes on Alan, he said" I want a trial" and a trial he had. A jury selected and opening arguments were made witnesses called and within two days the. The trial was over and the jury reached its. Verdict, guilty as charged.

The sound of silence was there for all to hear, Alan would not be a snitch a rat or a turncoat. He was doing what he had to do for him no matter what the consequences were. To this day all Alan can remember is the judge saying. Sentence you to 15-years to life in prison. Sheriff takes him away. First, it was out of the safety of the courtroom then off to Rikers Island he went.

INNER PEACE DESCENDS ON ALAN

After two years in a maximum-security prison where Alan survived without a major incident one day in the winter suddenly with his back against the wall something totally unexpected happened. He had been very involved in meditation and meditated once a day for at least an hour per session. He found himself more and more at peace with who he was, where he was, and what he was. This state of inner peace was new to him and it took a while for him to adjust to it and understand what had happened to him.

At first, he thought it was the effects of some drug,but then he realized he no longer took drugs. Then he thought no it's something else something profound is happening to me. As Alan meditated again the meditation experience took him to the answer. It was something in meditation not in a drug or a food or someone that awoke in him this new and profoundly mind altering state.

He realized he was now a different person. Fear his constant companion was gone. In its place was tranquility. He had gone deep down inside to his heart where God and love dwell- that is where. one finds peace, contentment, and ultimate freedom.

The more he meditated the easier and clearer the whole situation became. He accepted the consequences that had befallen him. He accepted responsibility for what he did in the past . He saw in himself a new and more actualized-realized person- the one he always wanted to be.

Alan reasoned that if he was the cause of his inner turmoil then he could be its cure. He could be the kind of person who is not suffering from inner turmoil and as such he no longer feels its pain. Since he was now not in need of something out there he was coming from a loving place and as such no longer would do the wrong thing.

It can be argued that because Alan took f
If we were to have taken a survey 99% of those asked would have turned in the supplier and faced those consequences whatever they would have been. They had to have been different and perhaps could have been more severe but we just don't know.

What we do know is that Alan received the coveted blessing; freedom from fear. He has not had a day of fear since and as this article is written, Alan is a happy, healthy peaceful person who is not tormented by his past. He no longer needs drugs to ease the pain because the pain is gone.

SELF INFLICTED PUNISHMENT

As Alan reflected on what he did and why he now believed he was wrong in following Howie and worse doing what they did. He did not want to get away with it all as Howie was doing with no remorse no conscience to bother him rather Alan may have in order to atone somehow someway punished himself.

When this insight took hold Alan realized it was thru meditation that he could stop punishing himself and start loving himself. If he was the problem he also was the cure. The cure came by and through meditation and it was in the meditative experience that he had that inner peace descended upon him.

Forgiveness then arises- what is it? why should one forgive themself and another? He realized now that he was aware of what he was and that person is gone, responsibility accepted there is no more to do. To Alan, he had to forgive himself first and not blame him. Second, he had. To know that he would not now or in the future do the wrong thing for the wrong reason ever again. Once he came to this opinion and he saw what he had become he radiated peace, love and contentment to those around him.

FORGIVENESS

Prisoners guards and others took notice- he looked the same but he was now a completely different person. He began to get attention for this condition in a good way. No one tried to get over on him, he was not tempted by doing something wrong he was on the right path for the right reason.

After spending 5 years in prison Alan got from the governor of my executive clemency. He was set free from. Prison and now lives in Riverdale in a modest apartment overlooking the Hudson River.

Occasionally he uses his skills and talents to help others who are in mental pain and is almost always very successful.

THE 3 "IN"S WHICH CREATES THE SOLUTION

1. INQUIRY - keep as is accepted for. Where one erred, why, and how. Inquiry is facing the truth no matter where it leads and being true is the same as being aware of oneself. This is paramount to good mental health.

2. INSIGHT- Going within, penetrating the fog of denial and/or fear allows one to find the truth which when found is the key to insight. Once discovered, one can say "oh yes, now I recognize who I was when I did it, what I did that was wrong, why I did those things; and all to show me the way home";

3. INTEGRITY- Once one and two are resolved, integrity is what is left. Integrity means I can be trusted to do the right thing for the right reason. I am a righteous person; I can be counted on.

CONCLUSION

Alan discovered that going within is the best path to finding inner peace. It is in inner peace that one finds not only oneself but God and love. People in love do not do harmful things to each other, people who find god know right from wrong and find in themselves what they cannot find out there in a drink a drug or a cookie.

Alan made ass decision many years ago to come to the aid of Wisey when none of his other friends. Would he go there fearless of the consequences? He made the same decision here for himself.

Who would not want to find God? love and inner peace? We all do but none of us have to pay the price Alan did rather all we have to do is go deep within and meditate and we will find love God and inner peace.

Alan went from an average non descript young boy to something so extraordinary his story begs to be told. As kids Alan and Wisey were good friends. Alan was the comedian of the two and the trouble maker but when Wisey needed him the most (the fight) Alan was his only friend to show up. After gradation from college. Alan and his new friend went into the stock market and made a fortune. the only problem was they did it were bestowed upon him in such numbers he felt out of touch with who he was, where he was and what he was. This. unfortunately was his undoing and remarkable downwood spiral then to such inner peace one marvels at the process and new found state. Alan was given a choice by the prosecutor, give up your supplier and become a Snitch or go away for life in prison and lose every material thing! Alan made the right decision for the right reason and now lives nobly, peacefully and tranquilly in Yonkers NRC having goten executive clemeney.

www.ingramcontent.com/pod-product-compliance
Lightning Source LLC
Chambersburg PA
CBHW061356050726
47595CB00005B/2277